The Organ Music of

The American Collection

ORGAN MUSIC OF INTEREST AND DISTINCTION
from the Fred Bock Music Companies

Fred Bock Music Company ◇ *Gentry Publications* ◇ *H.T. FitzSimons Co.*
Available at your local music dealer

Adagio (from Third Symphony) (JG0657) . . . . Camille Saint-Saëns/ed. Fred Tulan
All the Things You Are (JG0541) . . . . Jerome Kern/arr. Billy Nalle
    in the style of a Bach trio sonata
American Folk-Hymn Settings (F0623) . . . . Jean Langlais
    Amazing Grace, How Firm a Foundation, Battle Hymn, and three more
Ballade for Organ and English Horn (BG0881) . . . . Leo Sowerby
    (or clarinet, violin, viola)
Century of Czech Organ Music (Vol. 1–F0606/Vol. 2–F0607) . . . . ed. Karel Paukert
Concert Etude (F0634) . . . . Anthony Newman
Expressions for Organ (F0624) . . . . Jean Langlais and Naji Hakim
Folkloric Suite (F0604) . . . . Jean Langlais
Hymns of Praise and Power (BG0705) . . . . Frederick Swann
    accompaniments for 15 congregational hymns
Organ Music of Fred Bock—Vol. 1 Six Hymntune Settings (BG0889) . . . . Fred Bock
    Be Thou My Vision, Morning Has Broken, On Christmas Night, and three more
Organ Music of Leo Sowerby (BG0879) . . . . Leo Sowerby
    Carillon, Pageant, A Wedding Processional, and two more
Rhumba (JG0544) . . . . Robert Elmore
Rhythmic Suite (includes Pavane) (JG0546) . . . . Robert Elmore
Thirty Organ Bridges (BG0702) . . . . Fred Bock
    transition bridges and interludes for service playing
Three Carol Preludes (JG0691) . . . . Richard Purvis
Toccata on "Christ the Lord Is Risen Today" (BG0634) . . . . Diane Bish
Trumpet Tune (F0626) . . . . Jean Langlais
    a work for Trompette-en-Chamade
Variants on Hymntunes for Congregational Singing (BG0629) . . . . Fred Bock
    last-verse harmonizations on 14 standard congregational hymns

Gentry Publications

H. T. FitzSimons Company

Fred Bock Music Company

Dedicated to Robert and Debbie Koebele

Table of Contents

A New Name in Glory

Sw. :Flutes 8' 2'
Ch. :Flutes 8' 2' 1', Sw. to Ch.
Gt. :Prin. 8' 2', Sw. Ch. to Gt. 8'
Ped. :16' 8', Sw. to Ped.

C. Austin Miles
Arranged by Diane Bish

+ Sw. Reeds 16' 8' 4'

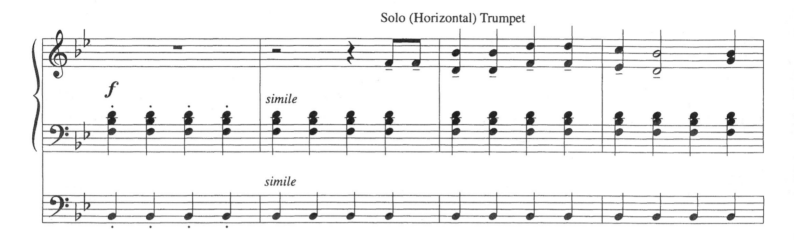

Solo (Horizontal) Trumpet

Echo   Gt.

Peace, Perfect Peace

Sw.: Oboe, Trem.
Ch.: Strings 16', 8', 4'
Gt.: Flutes, Small Prin., Ch. to Gt.
Ped.: 16' soft, Ch. to Ped.

GEORGE T. CALDBECK
Arranged by Diane Bish

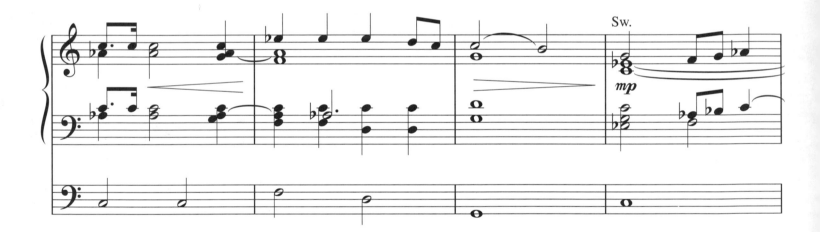

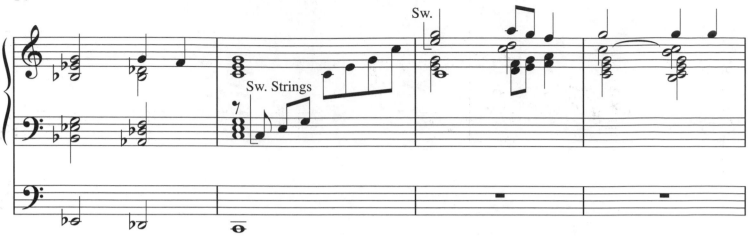

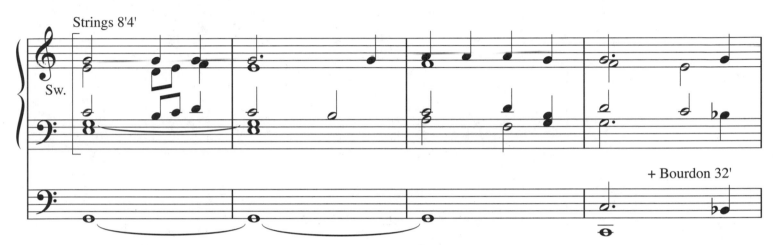

Jacob's Ladder

Sw.: Flute 8'
Ch.: Flutes 8' 4',Sw. to Ch.
Gt.: Flutes 8' 4' 2' Princ. 8
Sw., Ch. to Gt.
Ped.: 16'; Sw. to Ped.

Traditional
Arranged by Diane Bish

Andante - with movement

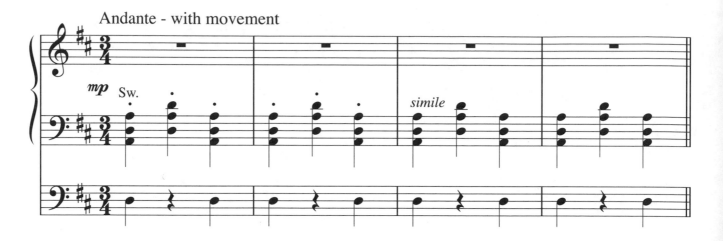

add Ch. Princ. 8'

add Sw. Flute 4'

mf
simile

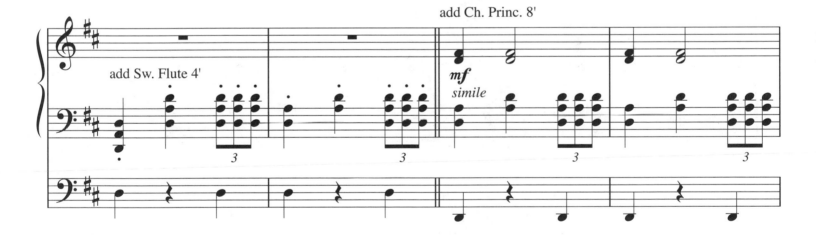

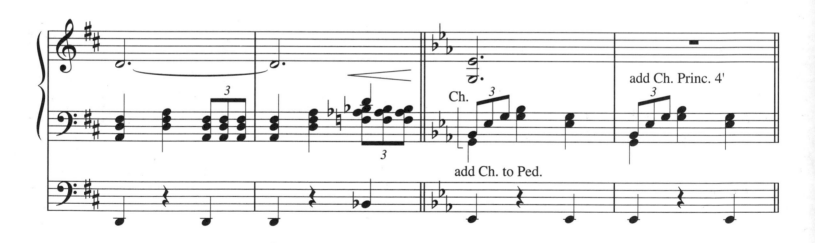

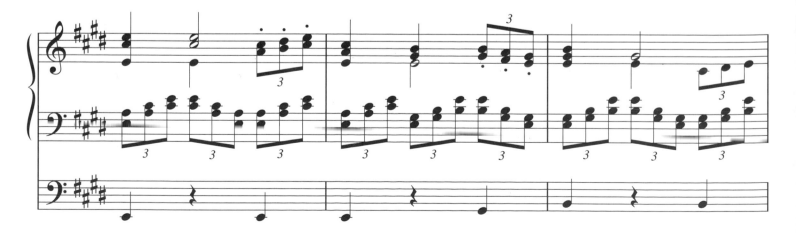

add Gt. Mixture

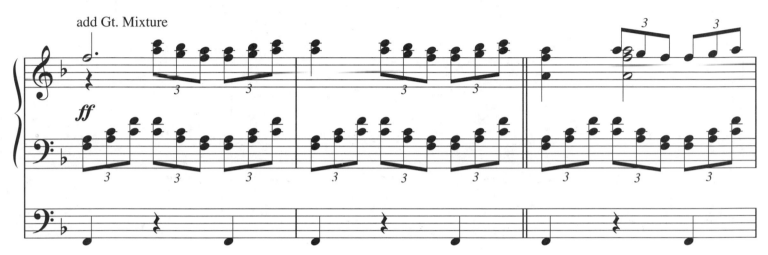

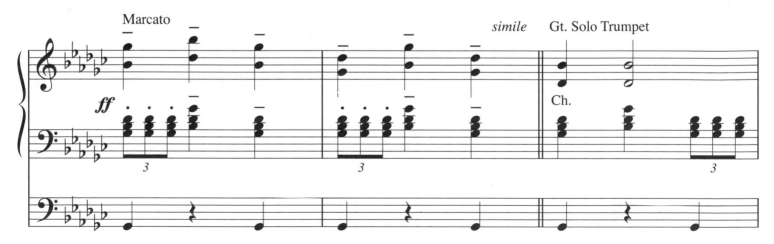

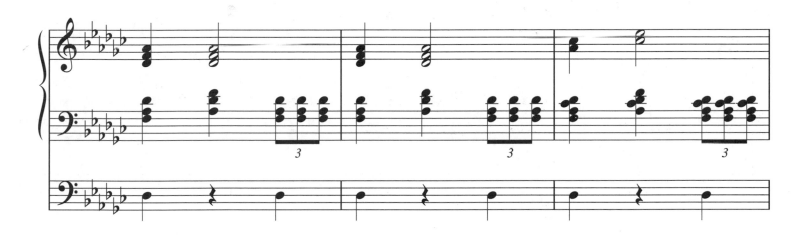

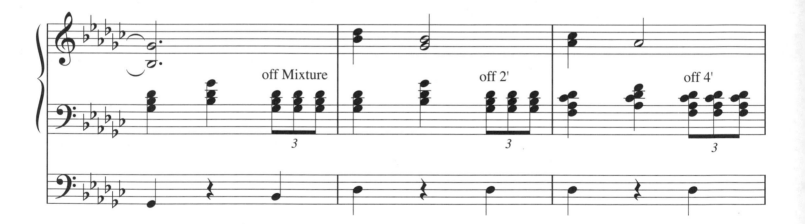

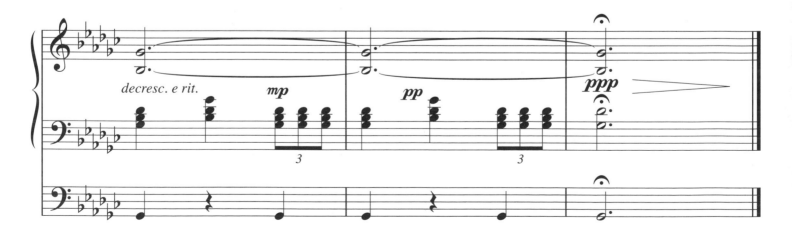

The Lord's My Shepherd

1			**2**	
Sw.:	Strings		Sw.:	Strings, Flutes 8'4', Prin.8'4'
Ch.:	Strings, Sw. to Ch.		Ch.:	Strings, Flutes 8'4', Prin.8'4'
Gt.:	Principal 8'(4')		Gt.:	Prin. 8', Sw.,Ch. to Gt.8'4'
Ped.:	16' Sw. to Ped.		Ped.:	16'8' Sw.,Ch. to Ped.

JESSIE S. IRVINE
Arranged by Diane Bish

Moderato - Expressive

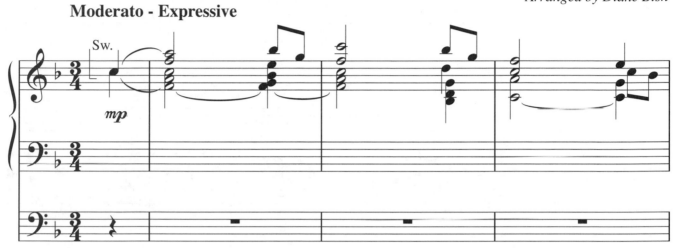

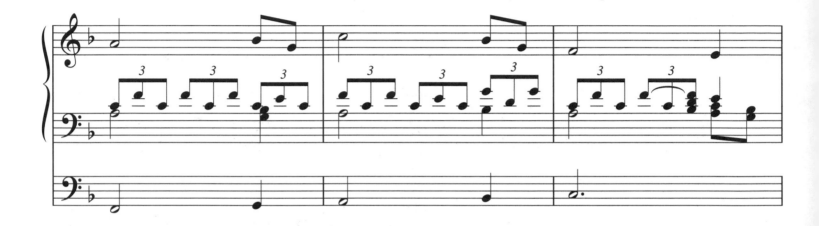

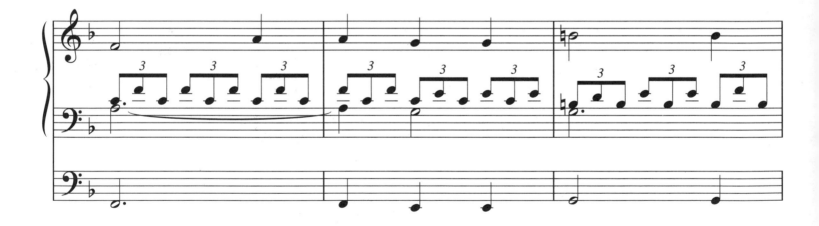

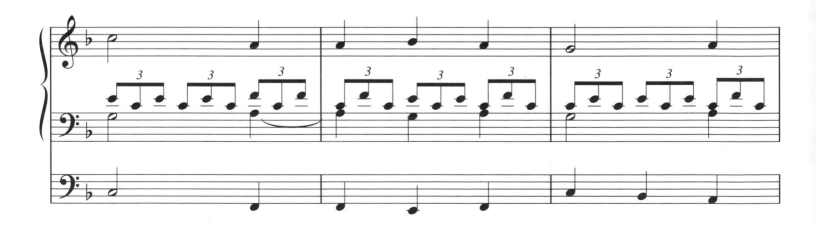

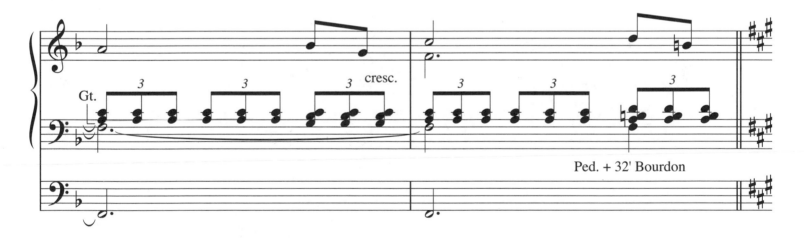

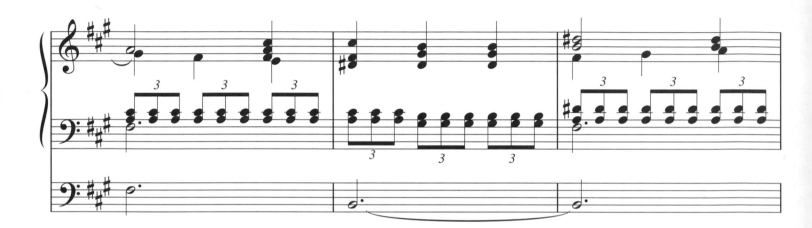

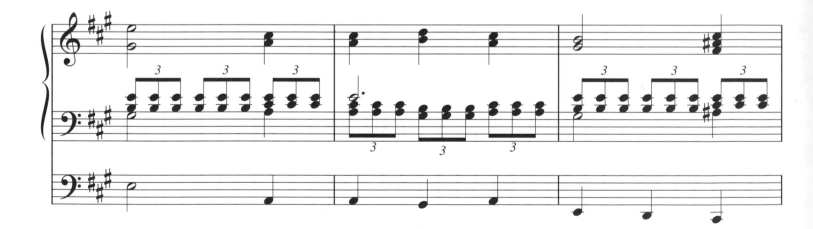

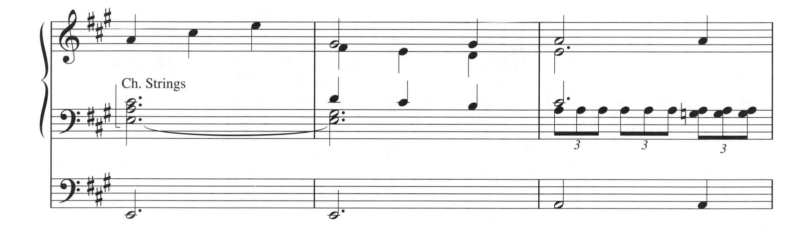

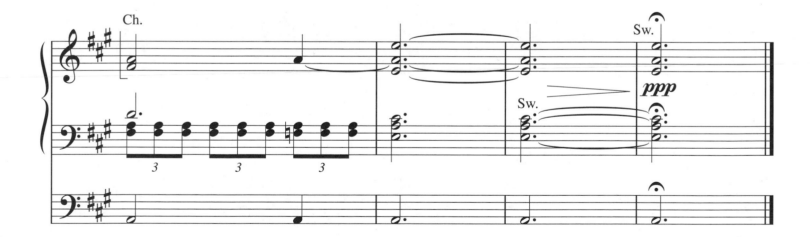

Come, Thou Fount of Every Blessing

Sw. Flute 8', 4'
Ch. Flute 8', 2', Sw. to Ch.
Gt. Principal 8', 2'
Ped. 16', Ch. to Ped.

NETTLETON
Arranged by Diane Bish

cresc. Ped. to Mix.

Gt.

Ch.

cresc. Ped. to Mix.

–Gt. Tr.
+ 8′, 2′, Princ.

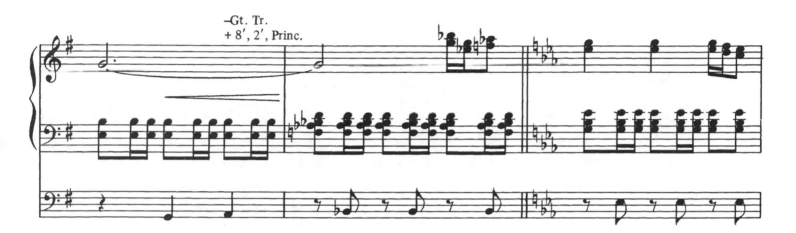

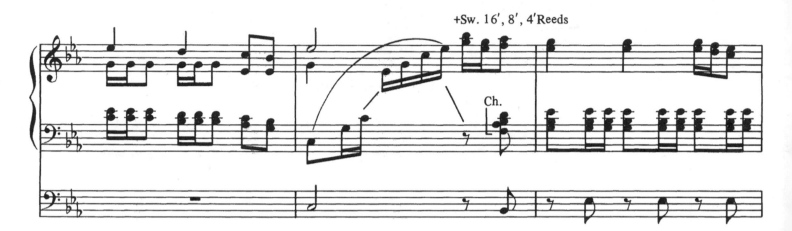

+Sw. 16′, 8′, 4′Reeds

Ch.

molto rit.

a tempo

fff